For

My Family

Introduction

This is the most complete book of the Aura you will find. It is the product of forty years research.

Following the easy steps explained here, you will be able to draw a colored diagram of your own aura. You do not have to be psychic or intuitive.

When you have finished you will be able to see yourself in a completely new light. You will see not only the glowing and kaleidoscopic colors of your aura, but also your strength of character, your emotional life, which factors are affecting your life and your connection to the spiritual realms

I am Jill Bruce, and I have been able to see the aura since I was born.

Since 1974 I have been a professional astrologer and clairvoyante. In each of the many thousands of readings I have given, I have produced a colored diagram of my client's aura. This has given me unparalleled insight into how the aura works, and I have written a complete, easy to use, compendium of my research for you to use.

- The aura contains the colors of the rainbow. Here I will show you how to interpret them. Their meanings change depending on which part of the aura they occupy, so you will have the most comprehensive list ever compiled to work with.

- Sometimes the aura moves or becomes distorted. You will learn how to perceive and interpret these anomalies.

- Emotions are very connected to the aura. From my in depth research on the aura's many sections, you will recognise how emotional blockages occur, and the effects they may have on your health.

- Your soul is mirrored in your aura. It leaves patterns within it. My easy to follow steps will teach you how to interpret these. You can now live your life in keeping with your soul's journey.

- Ancient religions of the world have always acknowledged a connection with our spiritual lives and therefore our aura. Here you will find listed, many associations such as angels, heavenly regions, chakras, astrology, the cabala and the plant kingdom. You may use these for your own healing rites, or those of others, should you so wish.

- These tables will also give you an insight into how you are a member of the Universe, and help you become aware of your networks to your many levels of being.

The aura is a wondrous thing; a collection of colors, light, and patterns which tell us much about ourselves and our surroundings.

If you wish to take part in this astounding voyage, learn about yourself, and maybe help others – read on........

Table of contents

The Aura

The Aura Your aura is a picture of you at this moment of your life. It contains all the conditions of your organs, emotions, thoughts, aspirations and traumas and triumphs.

You have a soul. It is thought your soul evolves over many lifetimes, and for this, it needs many different bodies. The one it is wearing now - yours - is constantly evolving for your soul to learn.

It has many things to learn, and cannot do all this in one lifetime. The soul chooses the lessons it needs to evolve before it enters a new body. When it has completed its lessons, it no longer needs a physical body and enters divine eternity.

These lessons will unfold throughout your lifetime. They are diverse, last different lengths of time and in varying intensities. Sometimes they are wonderful, like when you fall in love with the right person. Sometimes not so good, perhaps, if you go bankrupt.

The lessons are called *Karma.*

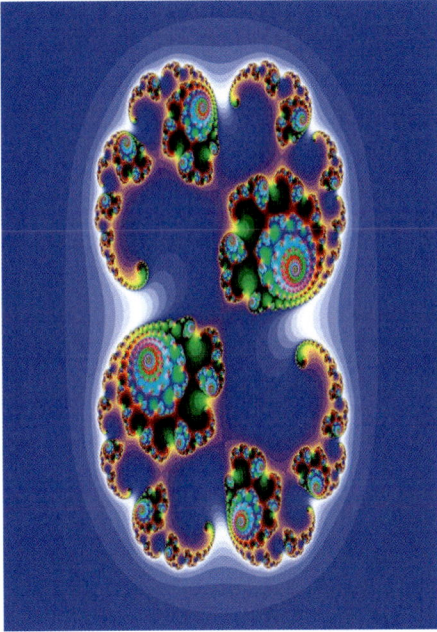

As they begin, a geometric pattern arrives in your aura, called a fractal. They are very beautiful and contain all the colors connected with the karmic lesson about to unfold.

The fractals make their way through your aura from the outer body – the 7th etheric– through the others towards your physical body.

They may not travel all the way to the physical body.

They may for example, stop at the 4th, which is the area connected to the emotions. This means you are about to have a karmic lesson where you must use your emotions, perhaps not in a way you have known before.

If you connect with the lesson and go through it, then the fractal disappears and that part of your karma is fulfilled.

However, if you cannot fulfil the lesson then a blockage in your aura where the fractal is trapped appears. This can then filter down to the physical body.

This is called 'dis-ease'. The karmic lesson is 'dis-eased' at its inability to unfold. Sometimes disease of the physical body can follow, as the blockage in the aura starts to alter the energies of the physical body.

It is our connection with the universal consciousness on many different dimensions.

The Aura – What is it?

This is the first question which springs to mind. Well, we have all seen medieval paintings of saints with golden halos around their heads. This is probably the closet pictorial representation you will get of it. It does contain many colors, and gold is the most spiritual one.

We all know we have a physical body. We can touch it and see it. So we are sure it is there. However, we have at least seven other 'bodies', we cannot see, they have their own properties, and work in tandem with the physical body.

These etheric bodies, as they are known, do not start on the outside of the body, rather flow through and around it. Together they form the aura which protrudes about a metre from the physical body, all the way round.

To understand how the aura can have a physical existence, it is good to imagine a hologram. It takes up a small amount of space, but a lot goes on inside it.

This is how the aura works. As well as all the etheric bodies having their own properties, there are several other elements all working independently, as well.

The most well known are the chakras. These are usually depicted as flowers, which have more petals, the higher up the dimensions, they are connected. These are described in more detail in the section on how to use the philosophical correspondences.

The aura *is not* what people see when they say they have seen a ghost.

When the physical body dies, the aura gradually disintegrates over a period of three days. Neither is it the soul; we cannot quantify the soul. It is thought to return to God after death.

The aura is very much part of our earthly existence. The physical body cannot exist without it, and the aura cannot exist without the physical body.

The aura holds all kinds of information; about our physical body, our mental processes, our spiritual feelings, and things which are about to, or already are, happening to us.

There is a faction of thought that says it is the aura which thinks, not the brain. This may well be so, because when watched clairvoyantly, the aura can be seen to change from any number of stimuli. It will turn olive green if they are being deceitful and red when they are having an argument.

What seems more likely, is the aura pans out information the brain cannot cope with. We know it is protective mechanism around the body, but it may also protect our emotions and thought processes as well.

It is surmised because we have many bodies, other than the physical one, these bodies can accumulate a great deal of information from many levels of existence. The brain could not cope with all that information in one go, so the aura only lets through what we need to use for our daily lives.

Learning to meditate on the aura, therefore, is very useful because it allows you to access much information and wisdom. This could be helpful in your daily life, but is otherwise panned out.

It is very easy to get in touch with an aura. Simply ask someone to stand in front of you, and then run your hands down the length of the body, but holding them about 18 inches away from the person. You may get a sensation of tingling, or it may be just a tiny change in pressure around the body.

Before you do, *tell yourself you can do it*. Acceptance of these principles is half the battle towards becoming intuitive.

Now, as you move your hands, you may become aware of patches of cold or heat. These are likely to be holes or tears in the aura, or patches of inflammation over the areas of the physical body, where there is likely to be disease. Disease can also show up in the aura before it manifests in the physical body.

If there is a hole, this should be closed. It can be basically done by running hands up and over the area – this is called massaging the aura – and filling the hole with golden thought light. Mentally see the person surrounded by light.

If there are any holes in the aura, energy will leak away and the person may feel permanently tired. Holes can occur at any place over the body, perhaps over one of the chakras. For example if the person is having a difficult divorce, the heart/emotional chakra will leak. Or if the person is having trouble getting through exams, the throat/communication chakra will be affected. We'll talk more about chakras in the next chapter.

Holes can occur also over places of illness – in fact it is vicious circle. The illness will not get better if there is a hole there, and holes due to emotional causes will have preceded the illness anyway. So, closing holes is very important. They can however, keep re-opening, so the healing process can take quite a long time.

The personality is another thing which can be assessed from the etheric bodies. Color combinations vary from person to person, in each of the etheric bodies. They are constantly changing due to many factors.

As you read on, you will understand the aura is never still, and that you as a person are constantly changing and evolving.

It is the purity and the clarity of the colors within a spectrum, which indicates the person's state in mind, body and spirit.

If the colors are jumbled up, then it indicates a confused state of mind. If the colors are muddy or pale it shows that the person is not living their life to full on that plane of existence. For example, green is the harmony colors, and should be lovely emerald shade. Often people who are not happy in what they are doing in their lives, will vibrate on a muddy green.

The aura is also a protective mechanism for the physical body. When it is sound and strong it protects us from debilitating forms of both disease and emotional disturbance. It helps to give us a 'thick skin'. However it can be weak and worn away in parts and this is why we feel vulnerable at times.

There are things which can cause holes in the aura. Two of them are drinking alcohol and taking drugs. The physical body doesn't quite know what to do with them and this causes a 'toxic' state within it. The aura reacts by lifting itself away from the physical body and a condition called 'displacement' occurs. The subject feels 'out of their head', and this can account for many other symptoms.

The Aura – What is it made of?
It consists of a subtle energy called etheric. This energy can be seen by sensitives. Photographs can also be taken of it, using special Kirlian photography.

It has not yet been described by physicists, but they are getting close. It is a very earthly thing. We cannot see electricity or radio waves, but we know they are there. So it is, with subtle energy.

Subtle energy is a very earthly phenomenon. The physical body cannot live without the subtle energy of the aura, and the aura cannot live without the physical body. When the physical body dies, the aura disintegrates over three days.

The aura consists of 7 etheric bodies. The first body goes through the physical body and extends beyond it by about 20 centimetres. The second body goes also goes through the physical body and the first body, and extends past the physical body by about 30 centimetres. This continues with the other bodies until the seventh body has passed through all the others and ends about 60 centimetres from the physical body.

At the front and back edges of each of the bodies there is a wheel of energy called a chakra.

They are usually depicted as being in a straight line from the feet to the head. These are situated on the feet, the pelvis, the solar plexus, the chest, the brow and the top of the head.

They run through the etheric bodies, and end at the front and back of each one. The base chakra has four sepals, and looks like a little flower. As they continue up the body these sepals double until you reach the crown chakra which has sepals which are believed to be uncountable.

They connect to the physical body through the spine and through the glands of the endocrine system.

They rotate, and open and close are associated with the emotions you feel.

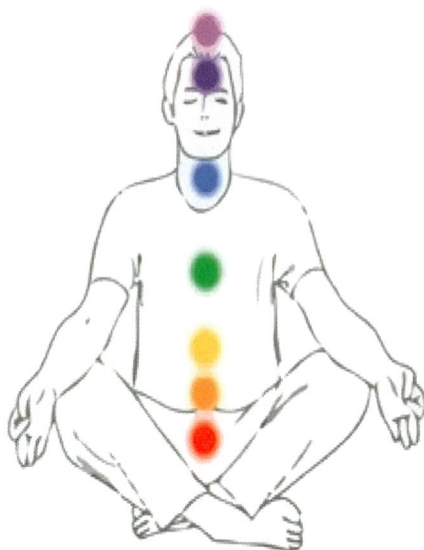

The crown chakra is connected to the pituitary gland,

the brow chakra to the pineal,

the throat to the thyroid,

the heart to the thymus,

the solar plexus to the pancreas,

the pelvis to the adrenals

the base to the gonads and the ovaries.

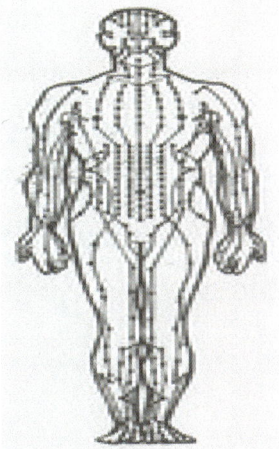

Running close to the physical body are lines of energy called meridians. These are lines of energy, which allow the balanced flow of subtle energy through your physical body, and so keep you healthy. There are many different lines, mostly connected to particular organs.

Within them are acupressure points. These are like little islands, or junctions, where the energy flows along the meridian 'roads'. Sometimes they become blocked. This can cause a problem in the physical body. It is these points that the acupuncturist will use in their technique.

Around the physical body, completely covering it, is a black line. This is the electro-magnetic field, which can be disturbed by both the environment and disease,

The Aura – What does it look like?

It is usually oval, and has many colors within it. Some will be more prevalent are than others.

These colors change very often, as the person's mood or state of health changes. The meaning of the colors makes up a large part of this book, because it is these which give the picture of a person's well being. They do not just act on the physical level, but on the mental and spiritual levels also.

When there are areas of 'dis-ease' in your life, your aura changes shape, and may get damaged or become distorted. When everything in your life is in balance and you are living a happy existence, then the aura is a delightful picture of a perfect oval, complete with dazzling colors. However, any karmic 'dis-ease' will show in the aura, and make that pretty picture, quite different.

Auric Damage

Etheric Bodies Problems

Wherever damage appears will have a bearing on the area of your life which will be affected. The first body is your physical well being, the second your will, the third mental issues and communication, the fourth the emotions, the fifth love, sixth karma, and the seventh, spiritual issues.

The most common are tears and holes. As subtle energy moves around the aura, it escapes through this damage. This can leave you feeling very tired.

It is important to close these up.

Sensing the aura is quite simple. Run your hands around someone's body about two feet away from them. You should sense a draught, or cold patches in places. These are tears or holes. By mentally filling the area with gold light, you will be able to close up the damage. It must be said these holes can open again, so they may have to be treated a few times.

There can also be blockages or areas which look denser than other parts. These are areas of 'dis-ease', and may be over areas of actual disease. Sometimes they can remain after the physical illness has healed, and sometimes will develop before a physical illness appears.

Etheric bodies can get mixed up. These indicate confusion about something in a person. For example if the second and third bodies are mixed together, this could mean that the person is having difficulties in deciding which avenue to take in their working life (ambition and communication).

Displacement can occur. This is when the shape of the aura becomes distorted. The most common, is the front of the aura becomes rounded, rather like a corpulent person. It usually means they are thrusting too hard in their ambition. They are leading with the heart area of the aura, literally pushing others out of the way.

This is often seen in business people, or those with a very stubborn way of seeing things. They are putting a great deal of pressure around the heart area of their physical body, and in all likelihood heading for a heart attack.

Sometimes the aura is displaced upwards. The person feels 'out of their head'. Alcohol and illegal drugs will do this, also some prescribed drugs. Being too spiritual can also cause this, as the person loses touch with the firmer issues of life.

Downward depletion, where the etheric bodies seem mashed into each other and indicates a heaviness pushing into the ground. This person is overloaded with negativity and so cannot vibrate in a balanced way. Long term use of alcohol, drugs, criminal activity and a simple refusal to sense the higher issues of life will cause this. They may also be violent.

Depletion of energy is a common problem. This can occur if there holes and tears of course, but also if the person is exhausted or ill.

Auric parasites are creatures which live on the astral plane and vibrate at a very low level of existence. They are very rare but can be seen in the auras of those who have had long term chronic problems reducing their life to a lower level. Things like addiction or criminality can do this, or those forced to live in an abusive situation.

Auric ulcers can occur in areas where parasites have been for a long time. They will precede disease in the area of the physical body where the ulcer lies. Often they can affect the liver. They are very difficult to heal.

The density of the color in a particular body will be in direct correlation to how a person is living their life. Lower density can be linked with general depletion of energy in that area. High powered colors, like too much red, can indicate an inclination to become over involved in certain issues.

Chakras can also become distorted due to the effect of emotions. They should rotate and open and close. However, dis-ease can sometimes cause them to completely close, or not be able to close properly, hence losing energy. Their shape may also become distorted, as can their position close to the edge of the etheric body.

Chakra Problems

The Chakras also will show distortion if there is dis-ease.

If they are blocked, this will indicate a blockage of energy flowing through the etheric body to which they are attached, and will have to do with the properties of that body.

For example, if the heart chakra is blocked, there will be a problem in the 4th etheric body, and therefore a problem with the emotions.

If the brow centre is blocked, then there will be a problem with the 6th etheric body, and therefore this will be a karmic lesson unfolding. As the pineal chakra is also associated with clairvoyance, this person's third eye could also be opening, and is being accompanied by 'dis-ease' of the subject in starting to feel all sorts of strange things happening to them.

The chakras should open and close, and rotate. If there is any 'dis-ease' associated with their particular properties, then these abilities will be blocked. It will be necessary to look at the etheric bodies to ascertain what the problems are.

The Colors of the Aura

The colors of the aura are usually placed, but not always, in the same spectrum as the rainbow. Therefore the first etheric body is predominantly red, the second yellow, the third orange, the fourth green, the fifth blue, the sixth indigo and the seventh, violet.

However, within each there is an extended spectrum of colors which can be viewed as 'normal'. These are discussed in the chapter on the etheric bodies of the aura.

But for a rule of thumb, the colors nearest the physical body are usually the life colors, red, orange and yellow. Further out are the harmonious greens of the emotional life, followed by the more spiritual blues and purples.

Red

Red is the life color. If there is too much of it the person is likely to be aggressive. If it permeates the entire aura, running across it in lines, then the person will have a magnetic personality. It is also the sex color, so there is usually more of it in young people's auras

If someone has a lot of red, and seems fairly well balanced, then they are likely to be enterprising and daring – and attractive to opposite sex. This is the color in the aura of many film stars. Bright red then, is a healthy balance.

Cloudy colors indicate things like greed and selfishness.

Orange

Orange is a color we associate with the Sun, and is the color of ambition. People with a lot of orange are usually in positions of responsibility, who are quite pleased with what they have done with their lives. Bright orange is a healthy shade. Dull orange can be thwarted ambition.

Yellow

Yellow is the color of Mercury, the god of communication. Very intellectual people have this color in abundance and also people who communicate on all levels. It is a very common color, and it would be unusual to find an aura without it.

Bright yellow indicates good thought processes, and a communicative, interested and optimistic outlook on life. Muddy shades indicate these processes have been blocked in some way, or they may be impractical dreamers. To find gold indicates the person may have developing soul qualities, becoming psychic.

Green

Green is the color of Venus, and is therefore to do with love and harmony. If there is a lot of emerald green it will indicate the person is full of ideas and is quite an individual. It always shows the person has reached a certain level of satisfaction with material life. There are a great many different shades of this color, all meaning various things, but from my experience olive green is deceit and dark green in jealousy.

Blue

There are also many shades of blue. I do not think I have ever come across as aura which did not display this somewhere. It is the artistic and spiritual color, and obviously, the more there is of it, the more the person displays these characteristics. The brighter the blue, the more positive the person, but it is common to find two or more shades in an aura. Pale sky blue, usually means healing abilities. Dark blue indicates emotional turbulence.

Indigo

Indigo or dark purple are indicative of highly evolved souls. One that has been reincarnated many times and it is a sign of wisdom.

Violet

Violet is a color I have rarely seen. It is the color of people with a spiritual, special destiny. It is the color of the initiate and the adept, and people who are meant to spend their lives in the counselling and guiding of others on a large scale, for example Mother Teresa. They are renowned for their unconditional love, and devotion to duty.

There are other colors which are not part of the primary rainbow spectrum, but which often appear in auras.

Grey

Grey indicates a rather red tape mind. One would expect it from someone who had worked in administration all their lives; a plodding unimaginative type.

It also occurs when someone has chronic illness, often back problems. It can mean depression when it appears close to the head.

Black

if you see this beware. It can mean that a person is negating a complete emotion and/or having evil thoughts. They may be actually capable of performing evil. Unfortunately it is also the color of cancer so be careful, because of course, these people are not evil.

Pink

Pink on the other hand can indicate the most sympathetic of souls, people like highly motivated nurses or carers.

It is however a most difficult color to define, and where it is placed within the aura is important. If it is near the physical body it is likely to be pale red, and can mean some kind of physical disability like anaemia or hormonal imbalance. If it is near the greens then it probably does mean a kind, sympathetic soul. If it is in the outer etheric bodies it can mean an adept who is probably mediumistic.

Silver

Silver is another color of Mercury and occurs in flecks, in aura of a talented communicator or mover. However, it can mean inconstancy and weakness.

Brown

Brown is the business man's color, and is usually the starting point of some ambition. However, brown patches on the inner etheric bodies will occur where 'dis-ease' has already, or is about to occur in the physical body. It denotes illness.

White

White is the psychic color, especially if preceded by a mixture of blue and green

There can be any color in any part of the aura, meaning many different things. These are listed in the chapter on etheric bodies in depth.

You may also become aware of a black line running very close to the physical body, all the way round. This is the electromagnetic field, which is an acute barometer of health. If this breaks down, there will be illness at that point

1st Etheric Body

This is a template of the physical body, and as such, has no particular mass. The colors are the same as for the 2nd Etheric Body, but you will find they are connected to the areas of particular organs.

Red	Alcoholism - Liver
Orange	Drug Addiction - Brain
Yellow	Liver
Green	Heart and circulation problems
Blue	Kidney problems, drugs - brain
Indigo	Thyroid and endocrine imbalance
Violet	Hearing disorder/schizophrenia - brain
Brown	Digestive and degenerative diseases - muscles
Pink	Hormonal disorder – usually ovaries, maybe other endocrines
Grey	Depression/Joint or back disorders – brain/particular limb
White	Temperature High – blots out other colors in first template
Black	Reversal of emotions- Heart

Cancer (may be striated with red) – over the area of physical body affected

2nd Etheric Body

Its color range is orange in its entire spectrum.

Chakra: Pelvic

It has an extremely complex honeycomb like structure through which divine energy is filtered.

Popularly this body is associated with ambition, but it is more complex than that. It energises the physical, mental and emotional patterns.

It is therefore of importance to healers as its mass can indicate areas of stress within the physical body. Here, the emotions alter the will; the stronger the will, the lighter the mass. Inertia produces dense patches through which the divine energy has trouble passing. Dowsing its density over different organs will give evidence of light and darkness, and positive and negative energies in each of the organs. There are directions on how to dowse in the section on how to draw a diagram of your aura.

Also, by dowsing the rainbow spectrum, it would be possible to ascertain the emotional and mental attitudes which affect the mass. For example, if a dense mass was vibrating on red, it would indicate anger or stress. If it was vibrating on indigo, it would indicate endocrine problems and or deep emotional turmoil, which it would be necessary to trace back through the outer etheric bodies.

Light diffuses from this body through the physical templates. Its clarity, density and purity are all indicators of what is happening. If the light streams through in its natural vibration, health and vitality are returned to the physical body. It is energised to carry out any tasks that the will requires. If however, any of these channels are blocked, then this can result in the de-stabilisation of the physical template and therefore, ultimately, the physical body.

The light is also received from the third etheric body, which is the mental body. Here again it is received from the will. Again, as with the physical bodies, if the light is unimpeded, the mental balance is obtained, if it is not, then mental imbalances of all kinds can ensue. This should not be taken too literally, unless there is serious imbalance in the third body.

The colors of the 2nd Etheric Body.

Red   Alcoholism

Orange   Drug Addiction

Yellow   Liver

Green   Heart and circulation problems

Blue	Kidney Problems - Deep emotional disturbance
Indigo	Thyroid and endocrine imbalance
Violet	Hearing disorder - Schizophrenia
Brown	Digestive and degenerative diseases
Pink	Hormonal disorder
Grey	Depression - Joint or back disorders
White	High Temperature
Black	Reversal of emotions E.g. where there should be love there is hate. Cancer (could be striated with red)
Mass	Honeycomb Structure
Density	Light
Planet	Mercury
Chakra	Throat

3rd Etheric Body

This is the Mental Body.

Chakra: Solar Plexus

Its color is yellow in the entire spectrum. Here the color is not so important as the density of the mass, and the direction of the spirals of energy.

Its mass changes according to mood, which may be affected by various pressures in the subject's lifestyle. Finances, relationships etc., mental pressures from work and education are also recorded.

When the mood is light and balances, then the mass is too.

However, negative emotions deepen it, and make it descent into the second body where it quickly alters the physical templates.

When the mass moves, it does so in spirals of energy. Negative energy produces a downward spiral, which pushes into the second body. But when positive spiritual enlightenment is sought, it streams in large loose spirals, upwards into the outer bodies.

It is the most comprehensive and complex of all the lower astral bodies. Spiritual lightness can affect its upward, spiral development throughout all the bodies.

On the whole, the outward permeation of this body is satisfactory. Its mass, permeating out towards the upper levels, brings a greater understanding of the higher and lower partitions of an issue, which produces a logical outcome.

Because this is the mental body, to produce a sound outlook on any issue, one must look in several directions before coming to a wise decision. The body, can then, protrude at will, into any other body to collect information. It is when the density of the mass becomes over loaded and it descends into the physical template that an imbalance has occurred. Because it is part of the mind, it can be used both consciously and unconsciously, for positive or negative effect.

However, too much upward development can be just as difficult as too much downward. It will help the individual to become unhinged from every day issues and over involved with spiritual matters. This is not recommended, the individual should vibrate equally on various levels – 'as above, so below'.

Its mass tends to resemble water gently swirling and eddying, but it can change to resemble tornado like tunnels, when negative emotions are involved.

The Colors of the 3rd Etheric Body

Red	Danger of Accidents
Orange	Perhaps over anxious to communicate
Yellow	Communication in positive channels
Green adultery	(especially olive green) jealousy, perhaps

Blue	Depression
Indigo	Involvement with inner thought - Psychological - Negative or positive
Violet	Presence of spiritual beings and spiritual evolvement
	Could represent mental problems if the person is not highly evolved
Brown	Lung problems - Difficulty communicating in business
Pink	Compassion
Grey	Depletion of energy
Silver	Quick thinking may be for good or bad.
Black	Murderous thoughts
Mass	Spirals of energy
Density	Light – permeates out to other levels
Planet	Mercury
Chakra	Throat

4th Etheric Body

This is the Emotional Body

Chakra: Heart

Its color is predominantly green, but it has the spectrum from yellow to the violet rays.

Its mass is like strands of cobwebs, very close together which form a lattice. The energy flow is in the form of clouds of emotions, which stream through the lattice like clouds of steam.

Negative energies slow or speed up the flow, causing blockages in the lattice work (rather like a slow driver on the motorway). These emotions can stay floating around here for years.

This body is more prey to auric vampires than any other, due to its open mass. When a blockage appears in the lattice work, auric vampires are allowed to enter. Because the blockage slows down the flow, this opens areas of vulnerability, which allow the invaders in. The aim for this body is to resemble a balanced summer day, but it often resembles a thundery sky.

One feels there is a kind of barrier between the 4th and 5th bodies; this may be due to the fact that the 5th body is the seat of love. Upward movement from the 4th could only occur in the spiritual forms of loving emotion otherwise the 5th body would be pushed into a lower dimension.

Clearly from the healing point of view, helping the patient to lift their negative emotions to the higher vibrations of the outer bodies is desirable, but obviously takes involved and experienced work. Unless the person can raise their emotions to their spiritual values, entry into the 5th body upwards, seems doubtful, except of course for the 3rd body, seeking information.

The Colors of the 4th Etheric Body

Red to excess	Anger - Oversexed, perhaps sexual problems due
	Possibly heart and circulation problems
Orange	Emotions being replaced by earthly pursuits
Yellow	Emotions being replaced by logic - Maybe scholar or someone involved in trickery.
Green	Emotions and harmonious life in positive action
Blue	As green, but tending towards the kind, sympathetic and artistic type Unworldly, perhaps a healer.
Indigo	Deep spiritual crisis of a karmic nature
Violet	Spiritual Awakening
Brown	Heart problems
Pink	Over idealised love – or love for a child – or pregnant

Grey	Heart broken. Deleted heart energy
White	Possibility of rape - this person has bad intentions. Not trustworthy
Black	Worst intentions
Mass	Clouds of energy
Density	Light becoming quickly darker
Planet	Sun
Chakra	Heart

5th Etheric Body

This is the seat of the power of love. Here it is beginning to be expressed in its highest form.

Chakra: Throat

Its color is blue, but it contains the spectrum from bright yellow/gold to violet.

Its mass is straight fibres, like thousands of optic lights. When they are straight and upright, this indicates positive, strength giving love. When they are flattened, they indicate the negation of love. Energy streams through the straight lines of fibres and permeates the emotional, 4th body.

Meditation on this body can bring one joy and ecstasy of God. Here one can learn the essence of forgiveness and thereby releasing oneself from life's traumatic times. Here one can learn that love in the greatest power in the universe.

It is interesting where it sits in the aura – the position between the causal and the cosmic. Here Man can consciously deny or embrace the love of God.

This body has the function of appreciation of the subtle areas of life, as the interface between the causal and the cosmic. Through it are channelled all forms of art and culture, in readiness to be transmuted from divine wisdom to earthly form.

Because it is the seat of love, it is the centre of mass religion. The transmutation of earthly desires into divine intervention. A two way telephone system from God to Man to God.

Its fibres are tentacle like, to catch any ideas, divine or earthly.

However, its fibres are easily flattened by negative emotions or the negation of love.

The Colors of the 5th Etheric Body

Red   If this is the correct hue, it could be love in its
             highest form

             As the color descends so do love motivations

Orange	Love transmitted to worldly pursuits for the good of humanity
Yellow	Difficult, lies, deceit
Green	If emerald, the person could be in love and have an excellent place in the world. Pregnancy. As the color descends through the green hues, so do the love motivations to jealousy and deceit, and over compensation through material gains
Blue	Correct - The higher the more spiritual the emotion.
Indigo	Karmic evolvement taking place
Violet	Spiritual identity unfolding - Spiritual love being given its highest form
Brown	Illness - Dependent or insecure
Pink	Psychic, mother love, pregnant, compassion
Grey	Loss of love
White	Dangerous, ruthless, rape, seduction - This color is carried in the aura of someone with bad intentions
Silver	Not to be trusted
Black	Murderous motivations

Mass	Straight fibres
Density	Light
Planet	Venus/Jupiter
Chakra	Heart

6th Etheric Body

This is the body of Karma. This is covered more fully in the next section.

Its spectrum is dark blue and violet

Chakra: Brow

The color of this body is dark blue to violet. The lighter the color, the more likely the person is to be heralding in disease.

The mass is very dense – this is why people are perceived to have a purple aura, other than any other color, and are called clairvoyants and old souls. This is usually true, because to have a highly evolved 6th body, would make you an old soul, i.e. someone who has reincarnated many times.

The etheric body seems to strike outward in shafts to other bodies as it carries the weight of karma in it. Rather like a crucifixion cross. Karma build up in geometric shapes and the color of the shape will give an indication of the karmic debt or lesson being absorbed. These geometric shapes make their way to other etheric bodies to unfold their karmic lessons. For example a yellow triangle in the 5th Etheric body, would mean a lesson of communication (see below), which is characterised with lie telling or deceit (yellow in the 5th body).

The Colors of 6th Etheric Body

Red	Very deep stress - Sexually orientated maybe - Bone problems
Orange	Negation of karmic patterns to pursue worldly aims
Yellow	Addictions, especially alcohol or gambling. No insight. Too mental to be insightful.
Green	A very young soul. Not developed
Blue	Artistic or medical type, healing, not worldly
Indigo	An evolved and positive position
Violet	Mistaken belief in spiritual identity. Person may have more faith than they should have, in what they believe.
Brown	Blocking out karmic evolvement with worldly issues, which is signalling the onset of physical disease.
Pink	An occult adept

Silver	An occult magician
White	Healer, psychic, seer.
Black	Imminent death. Cancer- Murderous thoughts and actions
Mass	Blocks and geometric shapes
Density	Heavy
Planet	Saturn
Chakra	Pineal

7th Etheric Body

The Divine Body

Chakra: Crown

The color is violet and is the link to the Divine. It is made of intensely white fibres which are very fine, and radiate through the color spectrum on a very high frequency, to appear violet. It has a million lights in it, which blink and are connected to enlightenment.

In some individuals the body is insignificant, in others it is the point of their evolvement. Only those with a true involvement with the divine will of God can use this body to its full potential.

It collects divine wisdom and stores it in time suspension until the karmic lesson unfolds. It takes many incarnations for it to evolve to its work of collecting, collating and teaching, through the individual experiencing the will of God.

As the body's attachment grows to the will of God, karmic lessons flow easier. The colors of the debt evolve from the rainbow hues of the fibres and are translated through the other etheric bodies into action, accordingly.

The Colors of the 7th Etheric Body

Red	Stress of the deepest kind. Mental chaos – danger to others
Orange	Listening to God's messages which are then transmuted into worldly wisdom
Yellow	Thief, deception, underhandedness, mental disturbance, schizophrenia
Green	Shutting out the world, in favour of their own inner world.
Blue	Healing, compassion, artist, doctor
Indigo	Old Soul
Violet	High Spiritual Evolvement
Brown	Deep, could be fatal illness

Pink	Medium, adept, psychic
Grey	Loss of spiritual energy and path
Silver	Magician Sorcerer
White/Gold	Sacred Soul, Jesus, Buddha, Mohammed
Black	Fatal illness, Cancer, Mass murderer – Hitler type.
Mass	white fibres
Density	very light
Planet	Outer planets, Uranus, Neptune, Pluto
Chakra	Crown

Karma

You will recall the 6th etheric body is the seat of karma

Karma is the lessons of life we choose for our soul's development. We choose what we need before we return to earth, (Malkuth) at the beginning of each incarnation, for our soul's development at that time.

How we handle each lesson indicates how much karma we gain or lose.

The philosophy of Karma is to lose as much as we can in each lifetime, so that we can ultimately fuse with the Godhead (Kether).

To lose Karma one needs to promote goodness and positive action, to gain it one needs bad deeds and negative action. It is like a pair of scales.

But it is not that simple

Karmic Lessons can be

1. New lessons for the soul
2. Half-finished lessons from previous lifetimes
3. Lessons not taken on board from previous lifetimes. i.e. held over
4. Taking up knowledge from a past experience so that it flows very abruptly back into this life, making a foundation for knowledge and/or work.

Karma also affects relationships and the interaction of souls with each other. Until we have nothing more to say to each other, the Karmic dance will continue.

Health problems often precede Karmic lessons, as the spirit goes into 'dis-ease' at the soul's demands. However, sometimes the disease itself can be a karmic lesson.

A therapist should be able to spot the karmic state, to understand it, and deal with it in the best possible way in the given time. It is important not to interfere with someone else's karmic path.

The patterns of Karma

Geometric shapes have a philosophy behind them.

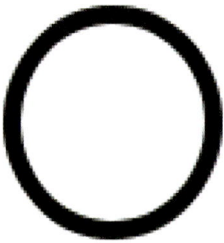
Circle

Circle

Indicates the subject is experiencing a lesson involving the unity of their life – how they assimilate the different aspects of their life into an integrated whole.

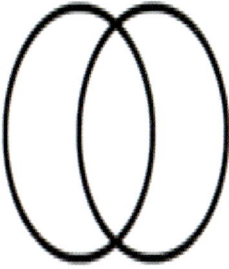

Vesica Piscis

Vesica Piscis

This indicates evolution from within, where the subject experiences the power of regeneration of some aspect of their life.

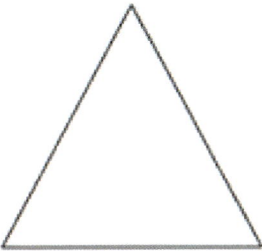

Triangle

Triangle

Here the lesson is to do with communication. If, for example, it presents in the 4th body it will be to do with the emotions, or if in the 2nd it will be to do with ambition and will.

Square

Square

The physical world and spiritual begin to fuse, and so the subject must look in several directions at once to complete the lessons which are becoming more complicated.

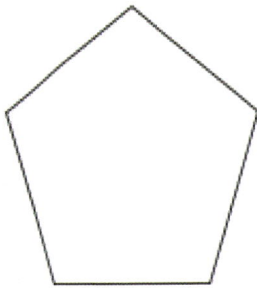

Pentagram

Pentagram

The physical, mental and spiritual aspects are fused together, in all forms of love, so the subject evolves to understand the subtler aspects of life.

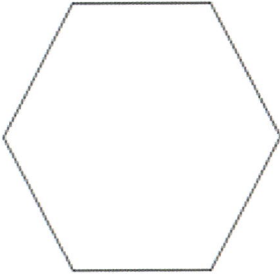

Hexagon

Hexagon

Usually indicates a very complex lesson, some of which the soul will have experienced before, and is adding to it within this lifetime.

Within these shapes are wonderful, intricate patterns, made up of many colors, and by identifying these shapes it is possible to discern more clearly what the unfolding karmic lesson is about.

By identifying the shape, the basic pattern within it and the colors, it is possible to identify quite closely how the karma is about to unfold. It can give all sorts of data: physical illness, mental imbalance, and the most useful, the spiritual pathway being signalled. This can be extremely useful to the subject, who can often be feeling very upset and confused by the unfolding situations in their lives.

When people are beset with these changes it can bring on intense stress and very often physical disease. Because they are used to looking for outside influences when karmic patterns occur, these influences do not always give full and satisfying answers. But when the subject is instructed to look inside themselves for the answers, and can be led to seeing the influences as tools for the soul's development, a different kind of behaviour becomes visible. They become interested in karmic unfoldment, and can become very involved with producing the best results for their own soul. This can only be beneficial to them and the rest of the world.

Also of importance is to ascertain whether these lessons are old, half-finished or new, how long they have lasted, and the time left to complete them.

Philosophical Correspondences of the Aura

How to use this section

Each of the etheric bodies of the aura is thought to be connected to higher planes of consciousness

Most religions have depictions of these different levels of being, and are usually seen as being an approach road to God/enlightenment/nirvana.

The following tables can be used for all kinds of healing and psychic work. If for example you wished to send healing to someone's 2nd etheric body, you would use the negative colors which are puce, silver, violet or blue, use them with the word of God which is Shaddai El Chai, and call upon the Aishim, which are the heavenly energies.

If you magically wanted to send them good fortune, to aid their career, you would again work on the 2nd etheric body, but do a ritual to the Moon, use the Virtue of Independence and meditate on the Visions of the machinery of the universe.

If you wanted to gain insight into your own Karma, you would meditate on your 6th etheric body, using the positive color indigo, and use the word of God, Yaveh Elohim. If you wanted to call for guidance on this Karma, you would call upon the angels of the Aralim, or the archangel Tzafkiel.

The Dimensions of Being

The aura is connected to supernatural planes.

The first, second and third etheric bodies are connected to the Astral Plane. This is the area which is most closely associated with the things which happen on Earth. It can be a place of deception, but then so can Earth. It is the home of the Akashic records, which are repository of everything which has happened on Earth.

The third is also connected to the Causal Plane, together with the fourth and fifth etheric bodies. This is a place of higher learning, and as the name suggests – causes things to occur on Earth.

The fifth and sixth are connected to the Cosmic Plane, in which the larger issues of life on Earth are decided.

The seventh is connected to the Divine Plane, of God.

The Astral is the dimension closest to us, followed by the Causal, the Cosmic and then the Divine, which is the seat of God.

Lower vibrational forms occupy the Astral, which is also a mirror of everything which occurs on Earth (Malkuth). The elementals exist on this vibration and are connected, as their name suggests, to each of the elements: ondines with water, gnomes with earth, salamanders with fire, and sylphs with air.

Fairies and many mythological beings are found here, and some souls remain here also.

Very negative life forms exist on the Lower Astral

The Causal holds higher beings – lower angels, smaller gods, lower demons, and higher souls.

The Cosmic holds the higher angels and archangels, archdemons, higher gods and cosmic souls who return to Earth only very rarely.

Positive and Negative Colors

These are very useful when used for healing or magic. Remember, when you meditate or think about healing, it is the negative color which attracts. So if you want to send someone healing – you send the negative color of the etheric body concerned, so that will attract the positive energies to that person. If you want to banish particular negative energies, you use the positive color. If you wish to investigate your own self, then use the positive color.

The Words of God

The Words of God have been used in the Hebrew religion for thousands of years. They represent a particular vibrational energy when intoned. These vibrations coalesce with the vibrations of different etheric bodies. They are particularly useful when used in connection with healing.

The Cabala

This is the Jewish representation of heaven and earth, and all its dimensions. It represents pure creative thought flowing from God, down through the spheres of the Cabala, or sephiroth as they are called. As these vibrations from God, travel downwards through the sephiroth, they collect information from them, as each as its own properties. These properties are dealt with in the next chapter

As the thought travels downwards it is said to lose its purity, as it is 'polluted' by these properties. In other words, it is becoming less divine, more earthly, and therefore, usable in this dimension.

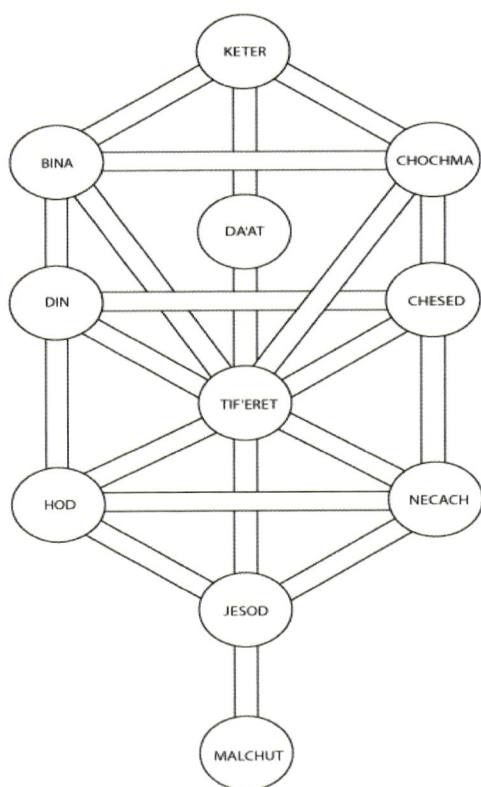

It continues to flow down through the sephiroth until it reaches Malchut (Earth) – and therefore, your brain. Once there, it can be put into practice in daily life. But you will have evolved in some way, to be able to be able to receive this message in the first place..

Astrology

Each of the planets of the solar system is seen in astrology to have properties which can directly affect people at certain times of their lives. They can also be viewed in this way, as being connected to different etheric bodies of the aura, and having a similar effect as would be displayed in horoscope.

Essential Oils

Essential Oils have properties which can connect them to all these philosophical correspondences. They can therefore be used in any healing techniques employed in this section. My book, 'The Garden of Eden' will help you make any further correspondences you require

The Heavenly Energies

The Heavenly Bodies are the angels and archangels which are connected to the different vibrational dimensions. The higher up the scale they are, the higher the etheric body they connect to.

Virtues and Vices

These are used as part of Cabalistic philosophy to describe the positive and negative emotions connected with each sephiroth. They can also be close to astrologic correspondences.

The Cabala

The Cabala is an ancient system of mysteries used by the Jews. Like most other esoteric learning systems it seems to have its roots in Stone Age times, and has been added to, and refined ever since.

We know that Moses was raised by the Egyptians and certainly studied their mysteries; how else would he have known how to turn his rod into a snake? So it follows that he would have contributed a certain amount of Egyptian philosophy to the Cabala while in the desert for 40 years. Legend has it, that Moses was given the Cabala, at the same time he was given the Ten Commandments on Mount Sinai.

Possibly its zenith as a world teaching came in the early 2nd century, when it blossomed along with other ancient philosophies in Alexandria in Egypt, where it was stored in one of the wonders of the ancient world, The Great Library.

Then as the first centuries after Christ were passed, the Hebrew religion was considered 'pagan', along with all other 'heretical' teachings. The Cabala went underground, and during this time, much learning was added to it. It was explored again during the Renaissance, and was of great interest to the thinkers of the time, and also by scientists, particularly alchemists.

At the beginning of the 20th century, The Golden Dawn, especially Israel Regardie spent considerable energy in incorporating it into magical systems. The Golden Dawn interspersed it with esoterics from around the world – astrologic, Buddhist, Arabic, Hindu etc., as they felt that these practices led to spiritual enlightenment. Contained in some classifications is what is known as 'The Angelics', a system of highly guarded and mysterious knowledge.

It is obviously a system from which meditation would yield wonderful results. First meditate on the spheres, then pathways and then working through the various properties of the sephiroth.

The Cabala has 3 pillars

Feminine/Severity/Left

Middle/Equilibrium/Middle

Masculine/Mercy /Right

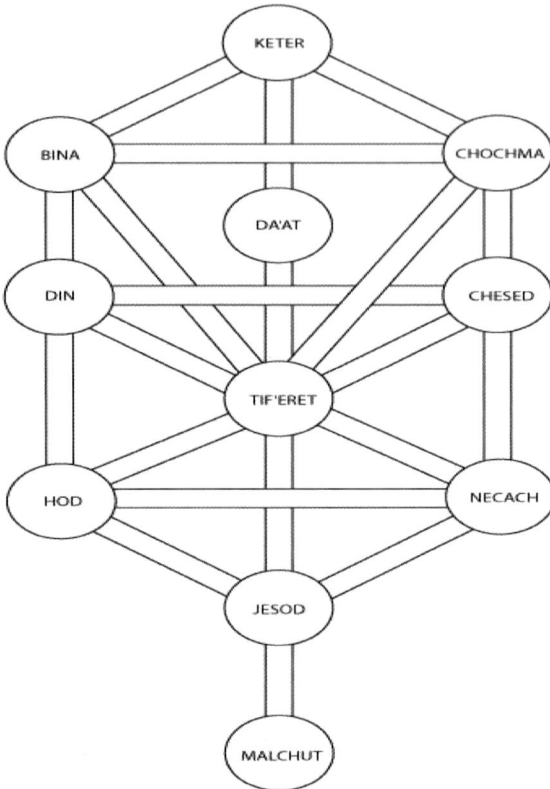

On each of these pillars are 10 spheres or sephiroth

Each sphere has many correspondences. The sephiroth are arranged in three triangles, with the tenth sphere hanging below the other nine.

The Cabala represents:

A picture of pure eternal light issuing from Kether and becoming denser as it flows towards the physical planes. This does not necessarily mean that any plane is better than any other – simply different. They are linked to the tarot packs, which gives further enlightenment as to their properties.

The sephiroth are also linked to the etheric bodies of the aura, and will channel their properties into our daily lives.

Colors of the Sephiroth

Malkuth	Citrine, Olive, Russet and Black
Yesod	Silver Violet or Silver Blue
Hod	Orange
Netzach	Green
Tiphareth	Rose Pink flecked with Gold
Geburah	Red
Chesed	Rich Blue
Binah	Black
Chockmah	Iridescence
Kether	Beyond Color

The properties of the Sephiroth

Ain Soph Aur light	which is nothingless, means, limitless
Kether	means the crown. Highest sphere, suggests kingly quality of wisdom and power. It relates to the 7th body of the aura.
Chockmah	means wisdom. The top of the masculine pillar it is the power of Kether in dynamic action, which stimulates and energies Binah. It relates to the 6th etheric body and has some of the properties of Saturn.
Binah	means understanding and is often known as the Great Sea or Great Mother. There is an analogy with human sexuality. Chockmah and Binah make force and form respectively. It relates to the 6th etheric body, and has some of the properties of Neptune.
Chesed	means mercy and compassion and is concerned with the up building of forces. However overindulgence can lead to vice. It relates to the 5th etheric body and has some of the properties of Jupiter.

Geburah	means strength, severity and justice. It breaks up, and tempers with justice the vices of Chesed. It is the corrective forms in its highest sense. Its negative forces are cruelty and vandalism. It relates to the 5th etheric body, and has some of the properties of Mars.
Tiphareth	Balances Chesed and Geburah and relates to harmony and benevolence. It is the higher mental consciousness, but can nurture or destroy. It relates to the 4th etheric body, and has some of the properties of the Sun.
Netzach	means victory and is the sphere of emotion. It is concerned in magic with elementals and nature contacts. It relates to the senses and passions – the thrill of living. At best it is the higher forms of unselfish love, and at its lowest is animal passion, sensuality, and living for kicks. It relates to the 3rd etheric body and has some of the properties of Venus.
Hod	is the reasoning mind. It is intellectual and incapable of higher emotions. It is the sphere of logic and insight, as well as

falsehood and trickery. It relates to the 3rd etheric body and has some of the properties of Mercury.

Yesod	means Foundation. The subconscious mind balances Netzach and Hod. It is the Astral light, impressionable and malleable. It indicates independence of your own path – but only if you can develop yourself. It relates to the 2nd etheric body and has some of the properties of the Moon.
Malkuth	The physical world, not related to any element, but related to the Earth.
Da'ath	Is the bridge, hidden by the abyss between Kether and Tiphareth.

Astrology - The properties of the planets

Each of the planets of the solar system has properties which are thought in astrology to affect each person in different ways, as they move through a person's horoscope.

The Sun   its qualities are hot and bright – warmth of emotion, great vitality and creativity, ambition and leadership, a concern with rational matters and the conscious mind. It rules the heart and the back.

The Moon   It embodies the female principle, and is in every way the Sun's opposite. It governs night, the irrational, the occult, depth of feeling and the unconscious mind – for which an archetypal symbol is the sea, which is actually governed by The Moon. The Moon's changeability links it with this trait and its traditional associations are purity and chastity. It rules the breasts, the alimentary canal, and the subconscious mind.

Mercury   This planet has a definite changeability of its own. But its principal quality is cleverness, which may take a variety of forms from academic brilliance to successful thievery and fraud. A mercury dominated person will be quick witted and ready tongued, and so will thrive as a communicator. He will also be successful in business and financial matters. It rules the nervous system, the throat and shoulder mantle.

Venus   Naturally a female planet, named for the goddess of love. She is therefore concerned with matters of love, beauty, sexual harmony and the fecundity of nature. Personality traits include gentleness and kindliness, gracefulness, warmth, sensuality and some artistry. But badly placed in a horoscope, the planet may produce selfishness, laziness and general lustfulness. It is also associated with worldly wealth. It rules the female reproductive system, the kidneys and the bladder.

Mars   The male opposite to Venus, with all the aggression of a war god: virility, extroversion and physical power. Energy, determination, courage and strength are the planet's most creditable feature. Crudeness, violence and destructiveness are the least. It rules the head and the blood.

Jupiter   The name of this planet is that of the king of the Roman gods. The planet is a benefic one, with regal and especially paternal qualities. Concerned with money matters and worldly success, Jupiter can do much good if well placed in a horoscope, conferring high rank, prosperity and good luck in any kind of gamble. It can also produce over-optimism, carelessness and a pompous manner. It rules the liver, gall bladder and pancreas. Sometimes the lower back.

Saturn   The planet of Karma. It herald's in life's lessons for us to work through. It can mean limitation and frustration, but it can also be the building blocks of one's life. It rules the skeleton and joints, skin and teeth.

Uranus   This is the planet associated with television, computers, air travel, rebellion and change. Independence of spirit will be evident, and ideals of democracy and freedom. It rules the circulation system and the rhythms of the body.

Neptune   The most unpredictable planet, related to gases, oil the sea, intuition and the unseen, and religion. There can be intense glamour, but also a need to escape as Neptune rules addictions of all kinds. It also rules the brain.

Pluto   This is the Roman god of the Underworld, and so the planet is related to death and rebirth. It is associated with volcanoes, crime, big business and sexuality. It rules the gonads.

Philosophical Correspondences of the 2nd Etheric Body

Word of God	Shaddai El Chai
Sephiroth	Yesod
Planet	Moon
Heavenly Energies	Aishim – souls of fire in charge of forms
Color	Orange
Area of the Physical Body	Solar Plexus
Positive Color	Blue
Negative Color	Puce
Cabalistic Philosophy	Will
Virtue	Independence
Vice	Idleness
Dimension	Astral
Essential Oils	Bulgarian Lavender, Cade, Chamomile Roman, Clary Sage, English Lavender, Eucalyptus, Galbanum, Ginger, Grapefruit, Hyacinth, Hyssop, Juniper,

Lemon, Lemon Verbena, Lime, Mimosa, Narcissus, Neroli, Niaouli, Oregano, Parsley Leaf, Petitgrain, Pimento Berry, Rose de Mai, Rose Maroc. Rose Geranium, Rose Otto, Fennel, Tonka Bean, Thyme, Ylang Ylang.

If you would like further help with essential oils please refer to my book '*The Garden of Eden*'.

Philosophical Correspondences of the 3rd Etheric Body

Colors   Yellow in its spectrum

This body encompasses both the sephiroth of **Hod** and **Netzach**

Hod

Word of God	Elohim Tzaboas
Planet	Mercury
Heavenly Bodies	Archangel Michael and defenders of the right hand path
	Angels – Ben Elohim, Children of God
Area of the Body	The conscious mind
Positive Color	Yellow
Negative Color	Orange
Cabala	Logic and Communication
Virtue	Dishonesty
Dimension	Astral/Causal

Netzach

Word of God	Javeh Tzaboth
Planet	Venus

Heavenly Energies	Archangel Hamiel,
	Patron of the Arts
	Angels – The Elohim
Area of the body	The reproductive organs
Positive Color	Emerald Green
Negative Color	Emerald Green
Cabala	Logic and Communication
Virtue	Selfishness
Vice	Impurity
Dimension	Astral/Causal
Essential Oils:	Amber, Anise, Benzoin, Bulgarian Lavender, Calendula Absolute, Caraway, Citronella, Eucalyptus, Ginger, Myrtle, Lavandin, Lemon, Lemongrass, Rose Otto, Vetiver.

If you feel you would like extra knowledge of how essential oils can help you please see my book *'The Garden of Eden'*.

Philosophical Correspondences of the 4ᵗʰ Etheric Body

Sephiroth:	Tiphareth
Color	Blue
Word of God	Jehovah Eloah ve Daas.
Planet	Sun
Heavenly Energies	
Archangel	Michael and Raphael
Angels	Malachim
Area of Body	Heart
Positive Color	Orange
Negative Color	Yellow or gold
Cabala	Higher Mental Consciousness
Virtue	Devotion to the Great Work
Vice	False Pride
Dimension	Causal
Essential Oils:	Amber, Basil, Bay, Benzoin, Calendula, Caraway, Cassia, English Lavender

Philosophical Correspondences of the 5ᵗʰ Etheric Body

This body encompasses both sephiroth of **Geburah** and **Chesed**

Geburah

Color	Red
Word of God	Elohim Gibor
Planet	Mars
Heavenly Energies	Archangel Khameal – Avenger of the Wronged
	Angels – Seraphim, Fiery Serpents
Area of Body	Head
Positive Color	Red
Negative Color	Red
Cabala	Action
Virtue	Energy, courage
Vice	Cruelty, wanton destruction
Dimension	Causal/Cosmic

Chesed

Color	Rich Blue
Word of God	El
Planet	Jupiter

Heavenly Energies	Archangel Tzadkiel
	Angels – Chasmalism, the brilliant ones (instability)
Area of Physical Body	Liver, pancreas, gall bladder, back
Positive Color	Blue
Negative Color	Purple
Virtue	Strength in its highest form
Vice	Bigotry
Dimension	Causal/Cosmic
Essential Oils:	Aniseed, cajuput, chamomile maroc, dill, Melissa, rosemary.

If you would like further help with essential oils, please refer to my book 'The Garden of Eden'.

Philosophical Correspondences of the 6ᵗʰ Etheric Body

This body encompasses the sephiroth of of **Binah** and **Chokmah**

Spectrum of body – dark blue and violet and includes black.

Binah

Word of God	Yaveh Elohim
Planet	Saturn
Heavenly Energies	Archangel Tzafkiel keeper of the Akashic records and archangel of the archetypal temple
	Angels – The Aralim – Thrones which shield us from sorrow
Area of Physical Body	Teeth, skin, joints
Positive Color	Indigo
Negative Color	Black
Cabala	Wisdom, karma
Virtue	Silence
Vice	Avarice
Dimension	Cosmic

Chokmah

Color	Iridescence
Word of God	Yahveh
Planet	Neptune
Heavenly Energies	Archangel Ratkiel, guardian of the gates
	Angels – The Auphanium, the wheels
Area of Physical Body	Hidden Purposes of the Brain
Positive Color	Indigo
Negative Color	Black
Cabala	Understanding
Virtue	Devotion
Vice	None
Dimension	Cosmic
Essential oils:	angelica, cajuput, cassia, cedarwood, coriander, cypress, dill, valerian.

If you would like further help with essential oils please refer to my book 'The Garden of Eden'.

Philosophical Correspondences of the 7th Etheric Body

Sephiroth	Kether
Color	Beyond color. Tiny white fibres radiating out to violet
Word of God	Eheieh
Planet	Uranus
Heavenly Energies	
Archangel	Metatron
Angels	Chioth ha Qadesh.Holy Living Creatures.
Area of Body	Beyond physicality
Positive color	None
Negative color	None
Cabala	Divine Inspiration
Virtue	None
Vice	None
Dimension	Divine
Essential Oils:	Cedarwood, cypress

If you would like to know more about how essential oils can help please see my book *'The Garden of Eden'*

How to draw a diagram of the aura

You will need:

A copy of the diagrams given below

A box of colored pencils

A pendulum

A clipping of your hair, about a centimetre long, sellotaped to a clean piece of paper

Paper

Pen

If you have never dowsed with a pendulum before, it is remarkably easy. At first you might find it astonishing that an inanimate object can move on its own, but you will soon get the hang of it.

A pendulum answers questions.

It will swing one way for yes – maybe backwards and forwards

And one way for no – maybe from side to side

So, between your thumb and forefinger, hold the chain so that it is about five centimetres from your thumb to the top of the pendulum.

Ask it a question in your mind, that you are quite sure you know the answer to. Like, 'Is my name...........?' Whichever way the pendulum swings will forever be the way you get a 'yes' answer. It might be backwards and forwards, or side to side. It will never change.

Now ask, 'Is my name...........?' and ask someone else's name. The pendulum should swing another way, to give the 'no' answer.

You now can ask it any question and it will answer yes or no.

However, if you hold it over the lines of the etheric bodies in the aura diagrams, it will act a little differently. Carefully, and quite slowly let the pendulum trace the line of the etheric body. The pendulum may swing in little circles, or side to side.

What this is doing is about to give you information you need to proceed with your diagram.

To make a psychic connection between the pendulum and the diagram, place the clipping of your hair under the diagram.

Step 1

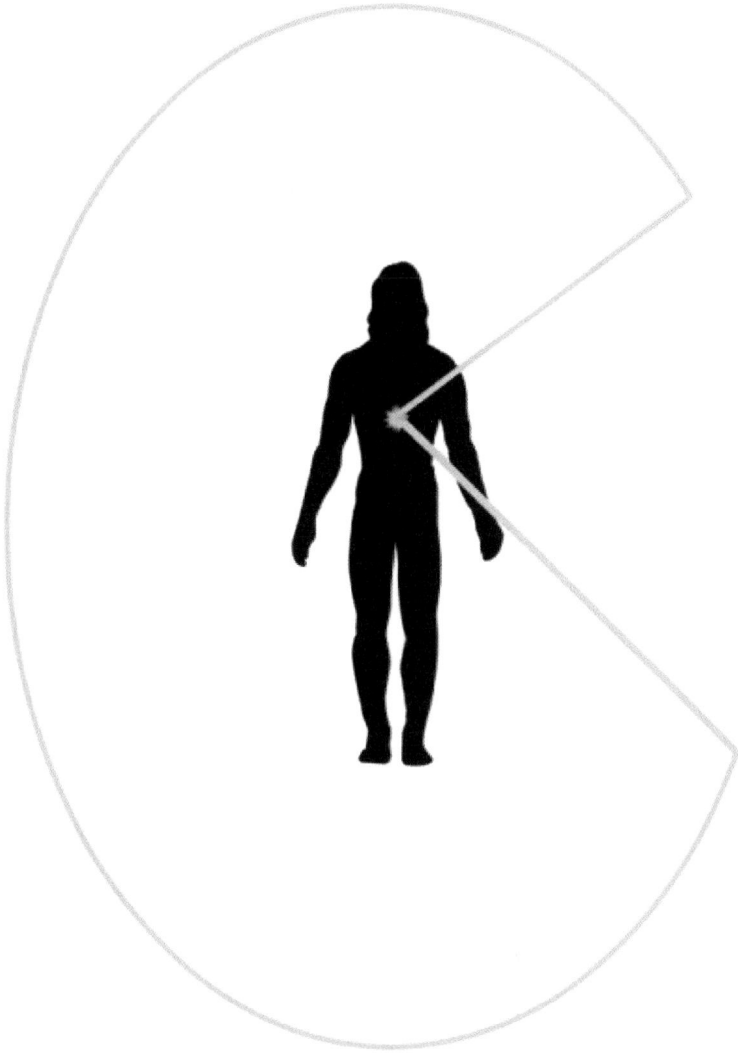

Diagram 1 will let you make a picture of where the tears and holes are in your aura.

Let the pendulum swing around the line edge, and ask in your mind for it to tell you where the tears are. It will swing in a particular way, and at a certain point, will either stop, or alter its pattern. This is the beginning of the tear, which you can now mark with an X. Continue on, and when you reach the point on the oval where the pendulum starts to swing in its former way, that is the other end of the tear. Mark this also.

Now take the pendulum and swing it gently over the body in the diagram, asking it to show you where the tear ends. Mark this with an X. Now draw a picture of the tear, by drawing one line from the first X to the third, and another line from the 2nd X to the 3rd.

This will now show you the area from which your aura is losing energy.

By sitting quietly and concentrating, it is possible to close up this tear. Imagine that place filling with white light, and the area closing itself up and healing. It may take several attempts, and you may have to concentrate like this for several days, but after a while, you will just become 'aware', that you are not so tired, and that you feel stronger. Your aura has healed itself.

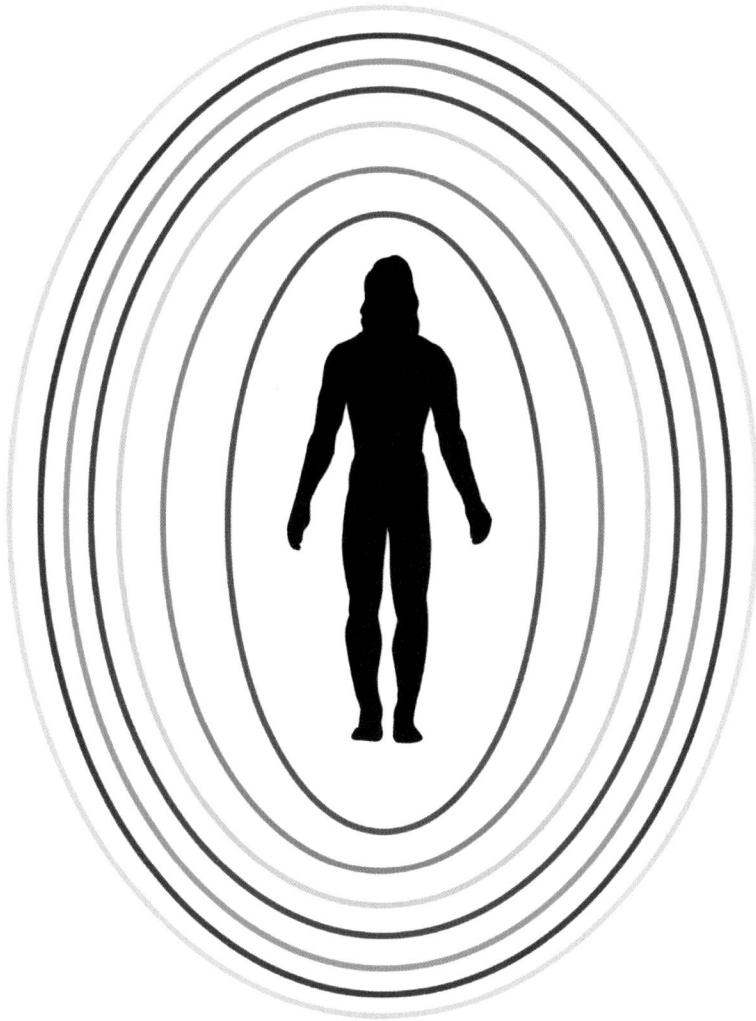

Step 2

Take a clean sheet of paper, put the hair clipping underneath it and ask the following questions:-

Are there any more tears or holes in my aura?

If so, where are they?

Are there any blockages? Do not worry too much about this, as when you come to the next step, the colored diagram should indicate where these are.

Are any of my etheric bodies mixed up?

If so, which are they? You will need to count back from 7 to 1 in your mind, so the pendulum can indicate which ones.

Is my aura displaced? If so, is it up or down?

Is my aura depleted? Again the colored diagram should indicate which areas are depleted.

Do I have aura parasites? This is highly unlikely unless you have been chronically ill for a very long time, a drug addict or an alcoholic.

If there are auric parasites, do I have an auric ulcer?

If you think you have either of these, pour white light, as described above, into them. The auric ulcer may take a long time to heal. If you are worried about this, then seek the help of a qualified healer.

Step 3

You can now complete Diagram 2 to make a detailed picture of the colors of your aura.

Again, place the hair clipping under the diagram.

Starting at the inner most oval, hold the pendulum as before and let it swing. When it changes direction, mark the place. Carry on around the oval until it changes direction again, and mark the place.

Now go to the colored pencils, and swing the pendulum gently across them, until the pendulum signals a particular one. It is signalling that the section of the aura you have just marked is actually the color of the pencil that the pendulum has just stopped at.

Take out the pencil and color in that marked section with it.

Continue from the last marked place, round the edge of the oval gain, until the pendulum, again changes course. This is your next section. Find the right color with the pendulum again, and colors it in.

Continue this way, until all the ovals have been colored.

Now go to the book section on the colors of each etheric body, and record what each of the colors you have drawn, mean.

You now should have a record of your health, emotions and personality.

Step 4

For your karmic lessons, hold the pendulum over the geometric shapes, and find which one it indicates for your unfolding karma.

Ask which body it is in.

Ask how long the lesson will last and is it coming in or going out

Then dowse across the spectrum colors in your pencil collection: red, orange, yellow, green, blue, indigo, violet, and find which colors are contained within the geometric shape.

Look up the body where the fractal is located, and then interpret it, by using the colors indicated there..

You now have a full record of your aura.

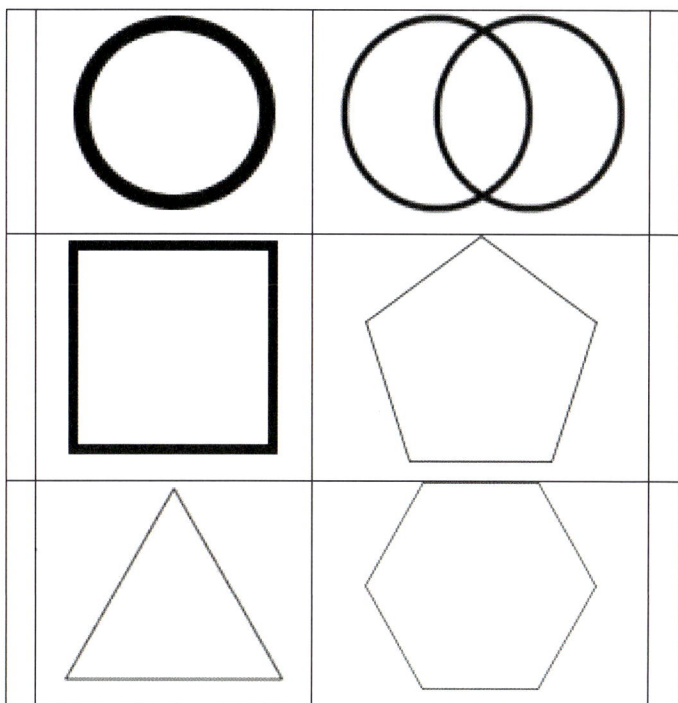

The Next Steps

If you feel you need more help with the information you have discovered about your aura, and would like to move towards a healing situation, I would recommend you take a look at my book 'Out of the Labyrinth'.

If you feel you need to explore your emotions, I would recommend *The Wise Woman's Journal*, by Angela McKay.

Conclusion

Well, I hope you enjoyed your journey, through the wondrous places to which your aura is attached. Did you ever think you were so complicated and brilliant!

If you have enjoyed the thought that you are connected to many different dimensions of being, there is a free download at *www.buildyourownreality.com/the-aura/* which shows the angelic realms of your aura. You can keep and enjoy it and refer to it, for future reference.

I hope you will keep in touch with the future books of Secret Knowledge, and please don't forget to leave a review on Amazon.

For further reading remember: For Healing – 'Out of the Labyrinth by Jill Bruce

For Emotions –' A Wise Woman's Journal' by Angela McKay

About the Author:

Jill Bruce BA (Hons.), LLSA, FECert. is an aromatherapist with many year's experience.

In 1987 she founded The Apothecary, which manufactures Clinical Products, Skin Care and Perfume from plants, and can be viewed on www.etsy.com/TheApothecary2

She is a former Vice Chairman of The International Federation of Aromatherapists, and a Principal Teacher for them.

She has been a professional astrologer and psychic since 1974.

She is a member of the Dowsing Research Group

She has two daughters and four grandchildren and lives in the Midlands.

Other works by the author

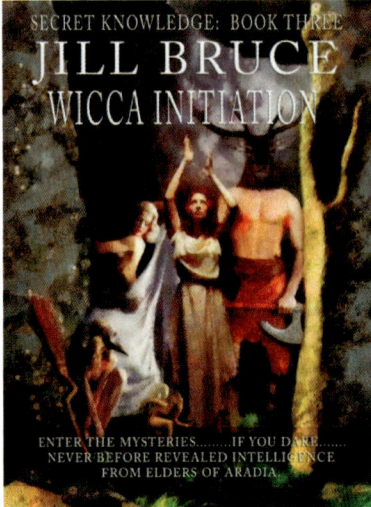

SECRET KNOWLEDGE: BOOK THREE
JILL BRUCE
WICCA INITIATION

ENTER THE MYSTERIES.........IF YOU DARE......
NEVER BEFORE REVEALED INTELLIGENCE
FROM ELDERS OF ARADIA

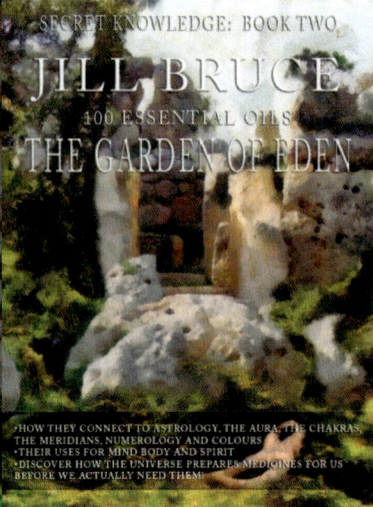

SECRET KNOWLEDGE: BOOK TWO
JILL BRUCE
400 ESSENTIAL OILS
THE GARDEN OF EDEN

•HOW THEY CONNECT TO ASTROLOGY, THE AURA, THE CHAKRAS,
THE MERIDIANS, NUMEROLOGY AND COLOURS
•THEIR USES FOR MIND BODY AND SPIRIT
•DISCOVER HOW THE UNIVERSE PREPARES MEDICINES FOR US
BEFORE WE ACTUALLY NEED THEM

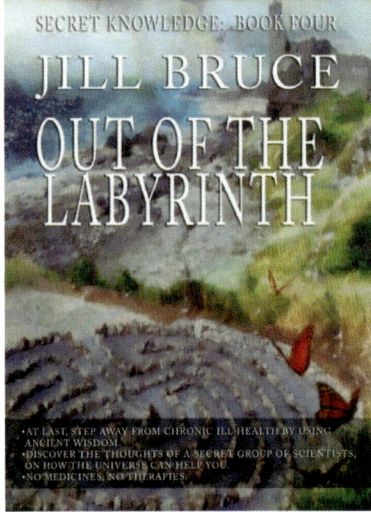

SECRET KNOWLEDGE: BOOK FOUR
JILL BRUCE
OUT OF THE LABYRINTH

•AT LAST, STEP AWAY FROM CHRONIC ILL HEALTH BY USING
ANCIENT WISDOM
•DISCOVER THE THOUGHTS OF A SECRET GROUP OF SCIENTISTS,
ON HOW THE UNIVERSE CAN HELP YOU.
•NO MEDICINES, NO THERAPIES.

Cover

https://www.elance.com/s/robertelsmoreimages/

Illustrations

hwww.elance.com/s/robertelsmoreimages/

Gil   Dekel . www.poeticmind.co.uk/humanity-appeal - Own work (enwiki)

Julia Set (highres 01)Public Domain

Disclaimer

by SEQ Legal

(1)   Introduction

This disclaimer governs the use of this book. [By using this book, you accept this disclaimer in full. / We will ask you to agree to this disclaimer before you can access the book.]

(2)   Credit

This disclaimer was created using an SEQ Legal template.

(3)   No advice

The book contains information about aromatherapy and the use of essential oils.The information is not advice, and should not be treated as such.

[You must not rely on the information in the book as an alternative to qualified medical advice from a health professional. advice from an appropriately qualified professional. If you have any specific questions about any medical matter you should consult an appropriately qualified professional.]

[If you think you may be suffering from any medical condition you should seek immediate medical attention. You should never delay seeking medical advice, disregard medical advice, or discontinue medical treatment because of information in the book.]

(4)   No representations or warranties

To the maximum extent permitted by applicable law and subject to section 6 below, we exclude all representations, warranties, undertakings and guarantees relating to the book.

Without prejudice to the generality of the foregoing paragraph, we do not represent, warrant, undertake or guarantee:

>   that the information in the book is correct, accurate, complete or non-misleading;

thatthe use of the guidance in the book will lead to any particular outcome or result; or

in particular, that by using the guidance in the book you will heal disease or work in any way as a cure for illness.

(5)   Limitations and exclusions of liability

The limitations and exclusions of liability set out in this section and elsewhere in this disclaimer: are subject to section 6 below; and govern all liabilities arising under the disclaimer or in relation to the book, including liabilities arising in contract, in tort (including negligence) and for breach of statutory duty.

We will not be liable to you in respect of any losses arising out of any event or events beyond our reasonable control.

We will not be liable to you in respect of any business losses, including without limitation loss of or damage to profits, income, revenue, use, production, anticipated savings, business, contracts, commercial opportunities or goodwill.

We will not be liable to you in respect of any loss or corruption of any data, database or software.

We will not be liable to you in respect of any special, indirect or consequential loss or damage.

(6)   Exceptions

Nothing in this disclaimer shall: limit or exclude our liability for death or personal injury resulting from negligence; limit or exclude our liability for fraud or fraudulent misrepresentation; limit any of our liabilities in any way that is not permitted under applicable law; or exclude any of our liabilities that may not be excluded under applicable law.

(7)   Severability

If a section of this disclaimer is determined by any court or other competent authority to be unlawful and/or unenforceable, the other sections of this disclaimer continue in effect.

If any unlawful and/or unenforceable section would be lawful or enforceable if part of it were deleted, that part will be deemed to be deleted, and the rest of the section will continue in effect.

(8)   Law and jurisdiction

This disclaimer will be governed by and construed in accordance with English law, and any disputes relating to this disclaimer will be subject to the exclusive jurisdiction of the courts of England and Wales.

(9)   Our details

In this disclaimer, "we" means (and "us" and "our" refer to) Jill Bruce of Buildyourownreality.com.

Printed in Great Britain
by Amazon.co.uk, Ltd.,
Marston Gate.